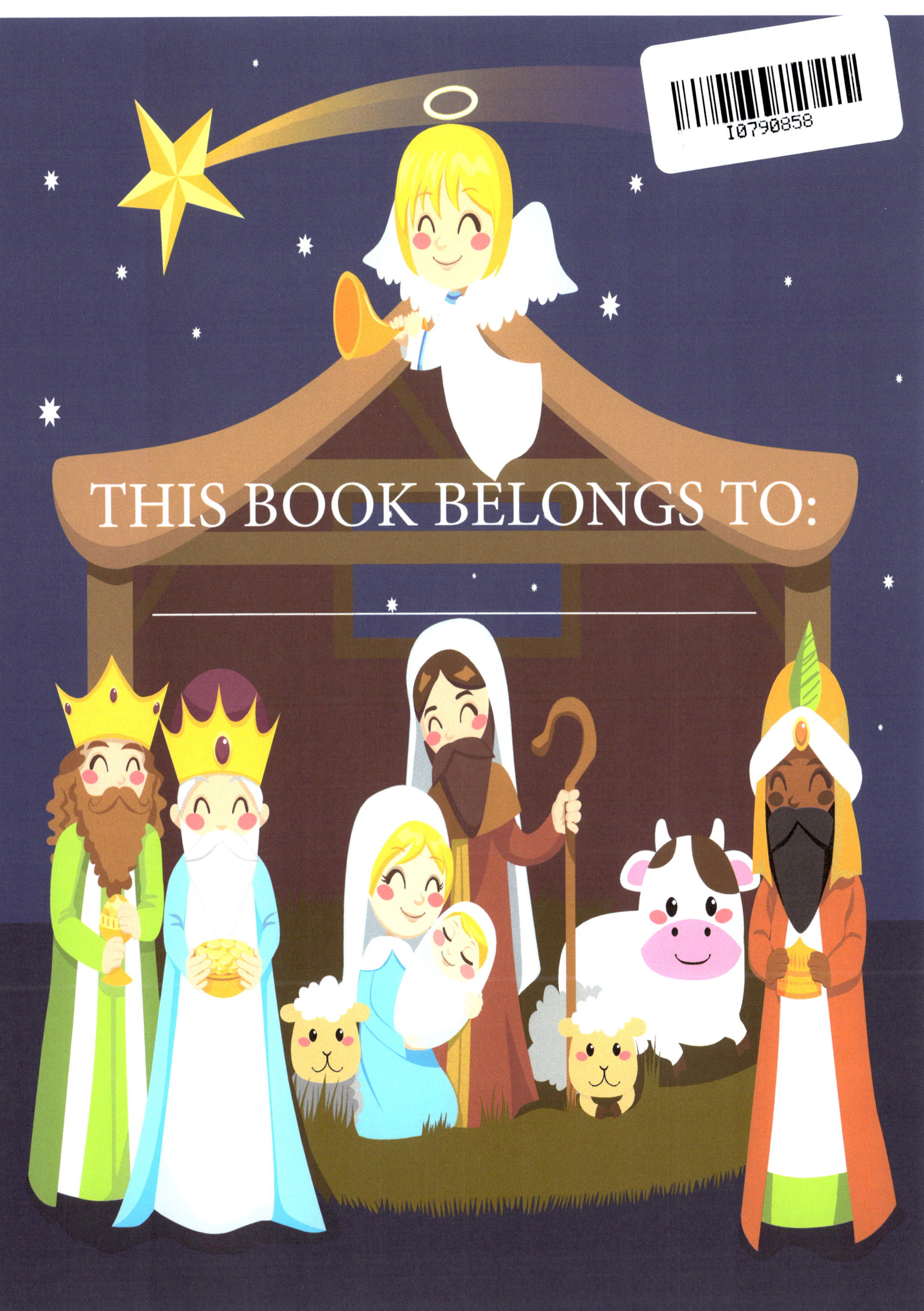

THIS BOOK BELONGS TO:

Tips for Using this Book:

1. You will need these supplies to get started: scissors, glue, dice, crayons, markers, or colored pencils, game board pieces, and extra paper.

2. Color in each day on the calendar (on the next page)as you complete each activity. Then glue the days in the correct order on another sheet of paper.

3. At the end of the book, extra pictures have been included for more nativity scenes.

4 You are free to do the book in any order because some activities/games may take more time to finish.

5. Have fun with family or friends as you do the activities and play the board games!

Advent Calendar

DAY 1

Cut and glue the pieces to create a nativity scene.

DAY 2

Name or make a list of the 10 things that don't belong in the scene.

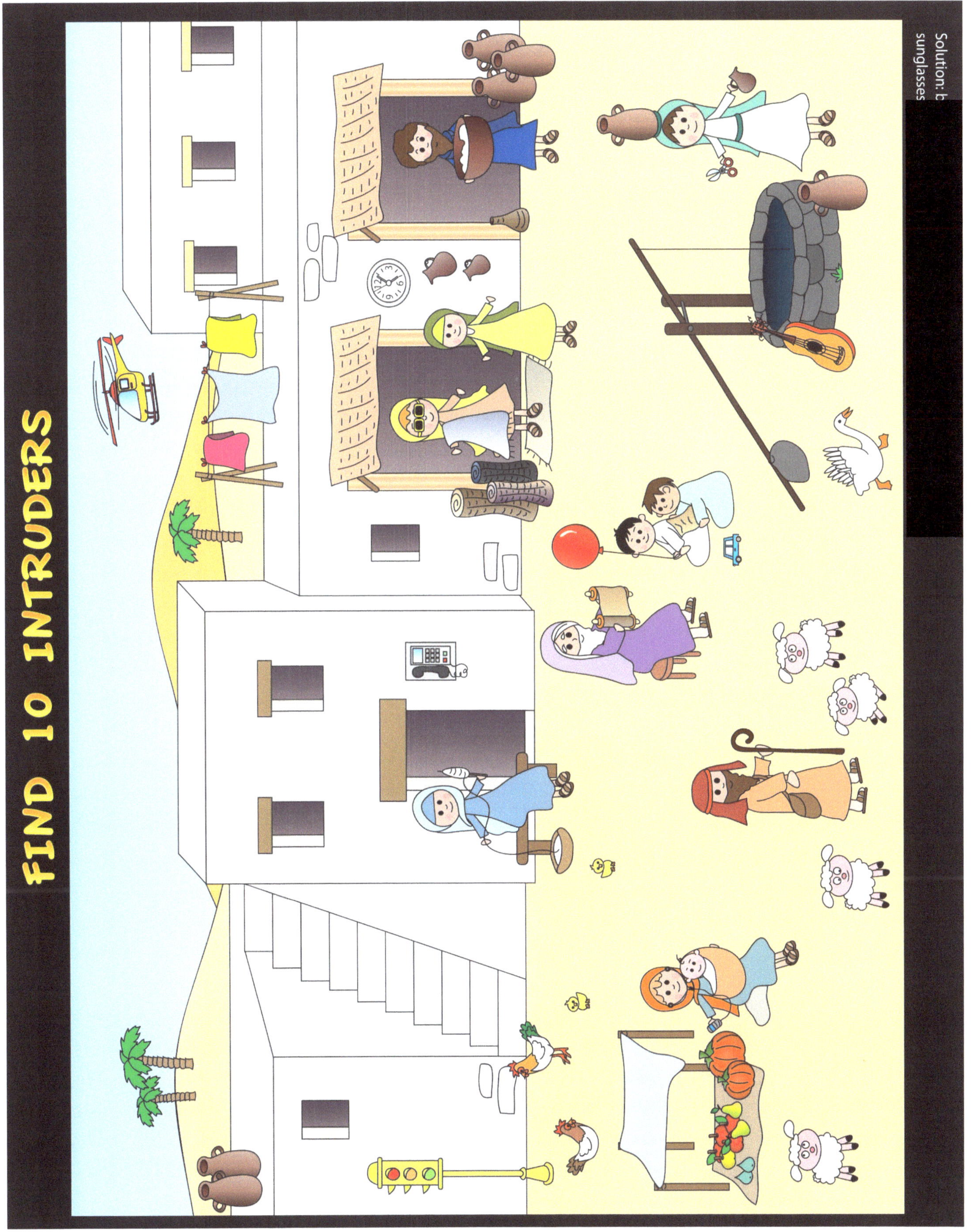

DAY 3

Help the angel find baby Jesus! Should she follow maze 1, 2, or 3?

DAY 4

Find the words in the word search to reveal the mystery word.

N	A	T	I	V	I	T	Y	M	S
S	J	K	I	N	G	S	S	L	T
A	O	O	B	B	E	T	H	A	A
M	X	C	S	I	H	L	E	P	R
T	Y	A	T	E	B	E	E	L	Y
S	R	M	T	E	P	L	P	E	E
I	A	E	U	H	M	H	E	G	K
R	M	L	H	E	G	O	D	N	N
H	J	E	S	U	S	M	C	A	O
C	D	R	E	H	P	E	H	S	D

DAY 5

How are the two pictures different? Name them or make a list of the differences on another sheet of paper.

DAY 6

Cut out and glue the game board pieces. Take turns rolling the dice to see who gets to the manger first.

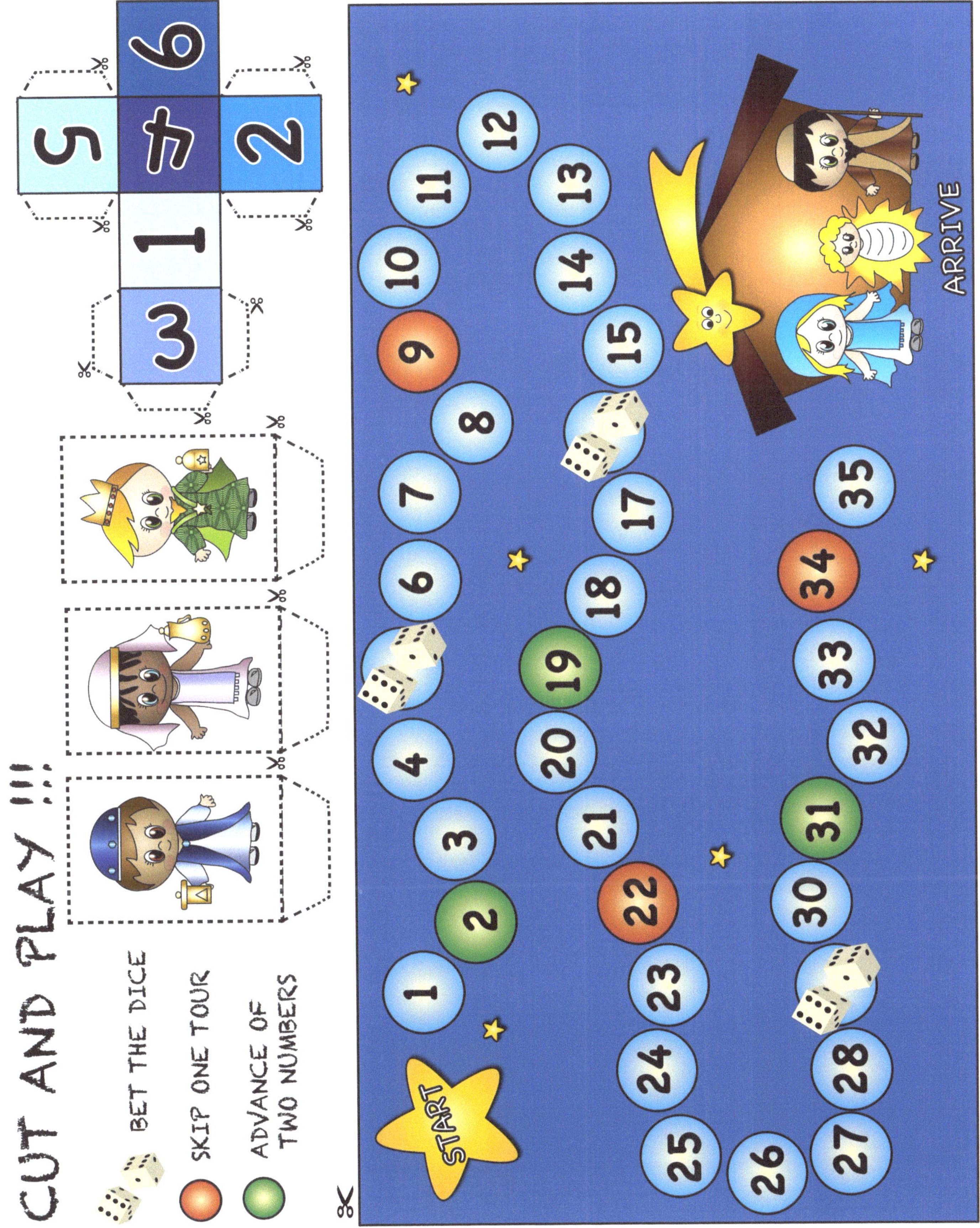

DAY 7

The Three Wise Men are lost! Help them each choose
the correct maze.

DAY 8

How are the two pictures different?
Name them or make a list of the differences on paper.

FIND THE TEN DIFFERENCES

DAY 9

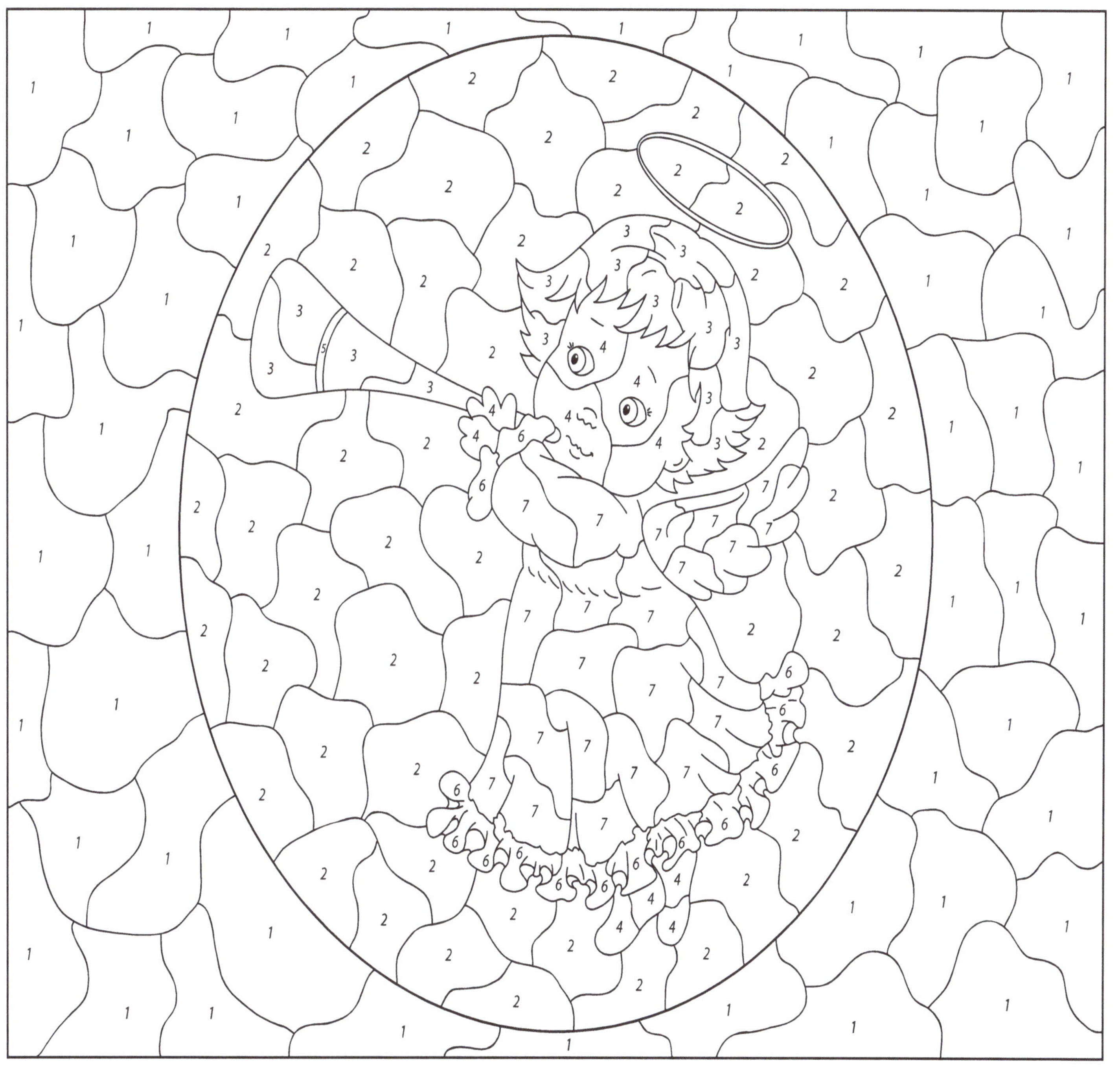

Color by number to finish the Christmas angel.

DAY 10

Cut and glue the pieces. You may use them for your nativity scenes or game boards.

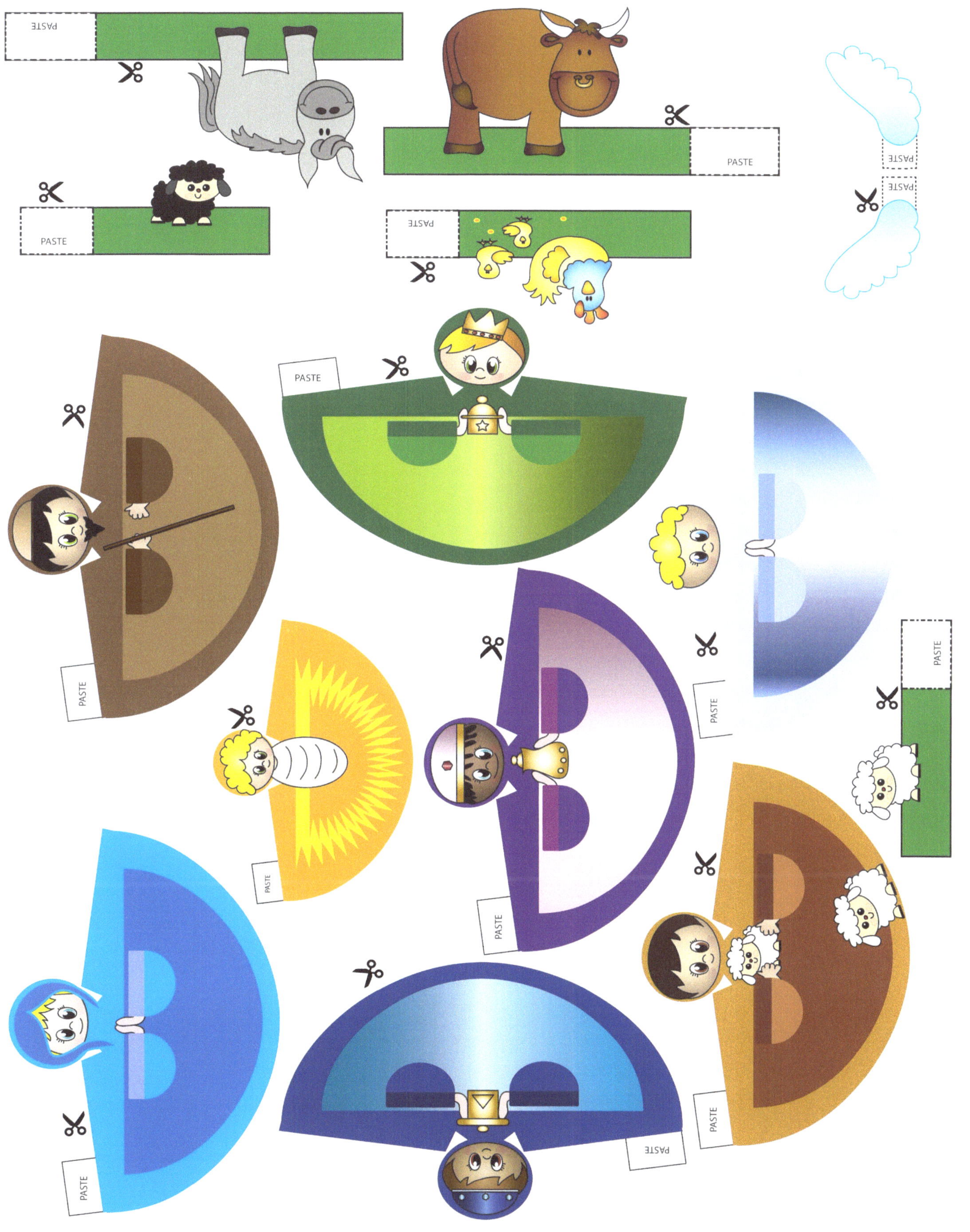

DAY 11

Help the shepherd & his sheep choose the correct maze. Should he take A, B, C, or D?

DAY 12

Roll the dice to find out how many spaces you move on the game board. Use the game board to practice counting, too!

DAY 13

Cut out the pictures and glue them to the numbered images.

DAY 14

Roll the dice to find out how many spaces you move on the game board. Use the game board to practice counting, too!

DAY 15

How are the two pictures different?
Name them or make a list of the differences on paper.

FIND 10 DIFFERENCES

DAY 16

Cut out & glue the game board pieces then follow the directions at the bottom of the page.

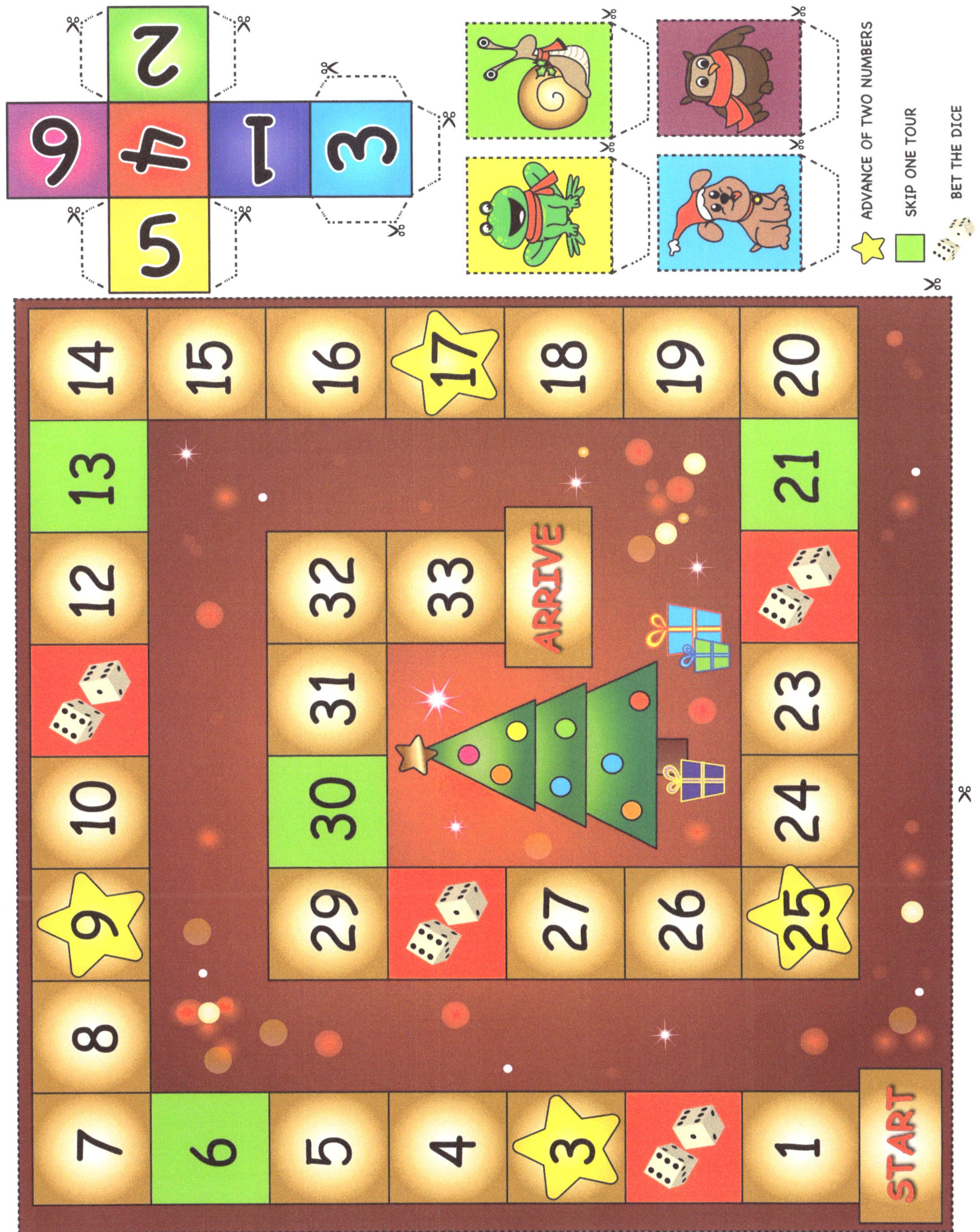

DAY 17

Write the word for each numbered picture. Decide if the word goes down or across. Hint: Count the number of spaces to help you decide where the word fits.

DAY 18

Add the total number of ornaments from both of the trees. Decorate the
blank tree with the total number of ornaments by using
colored pencils, markers,gel pens, or crayons.

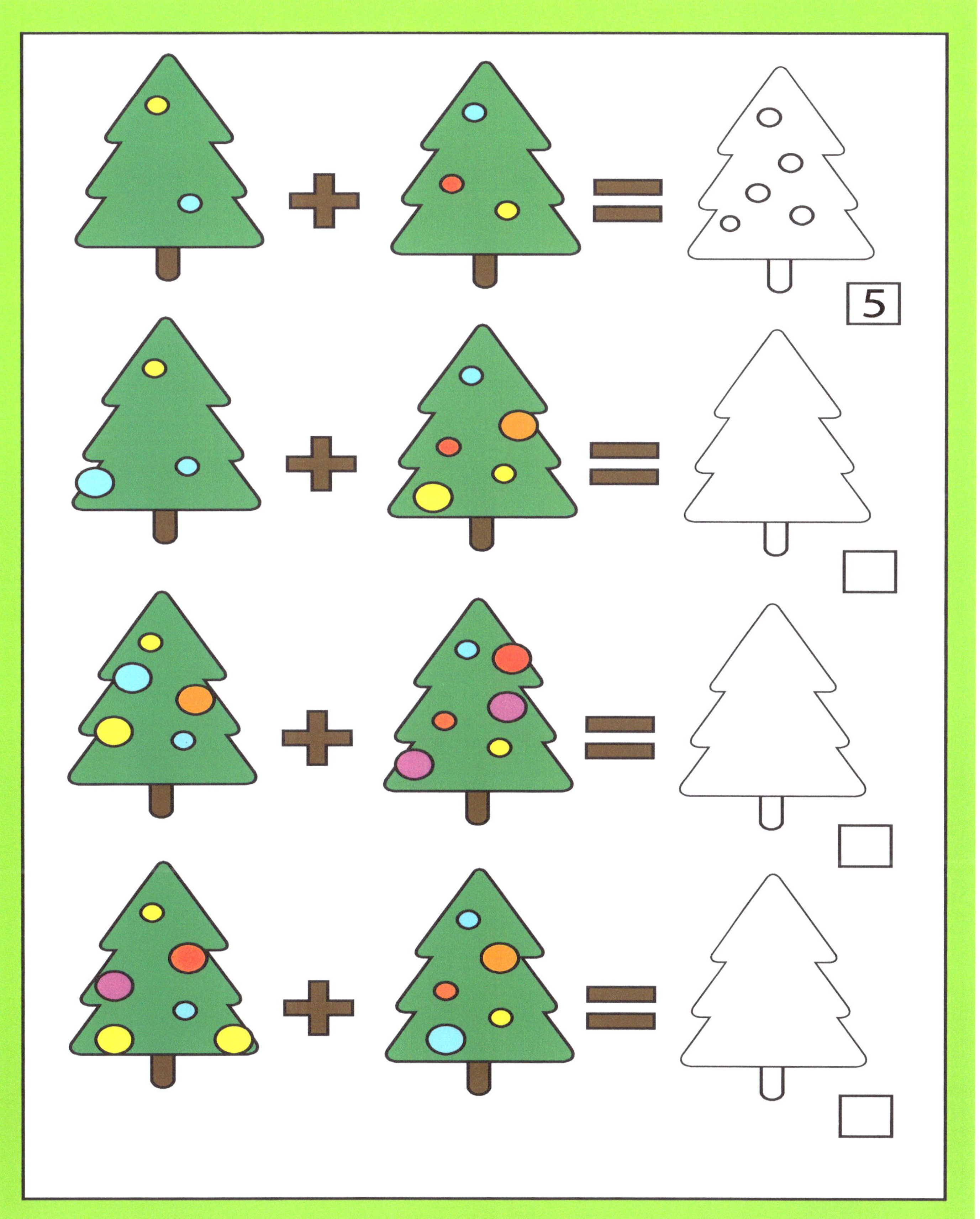

DAY 19

Help the Three Wise Men choose the correct maze to
find baby Jesus.

DAY 20

Color by number to decorate the Christmas tree!

Color by numbers

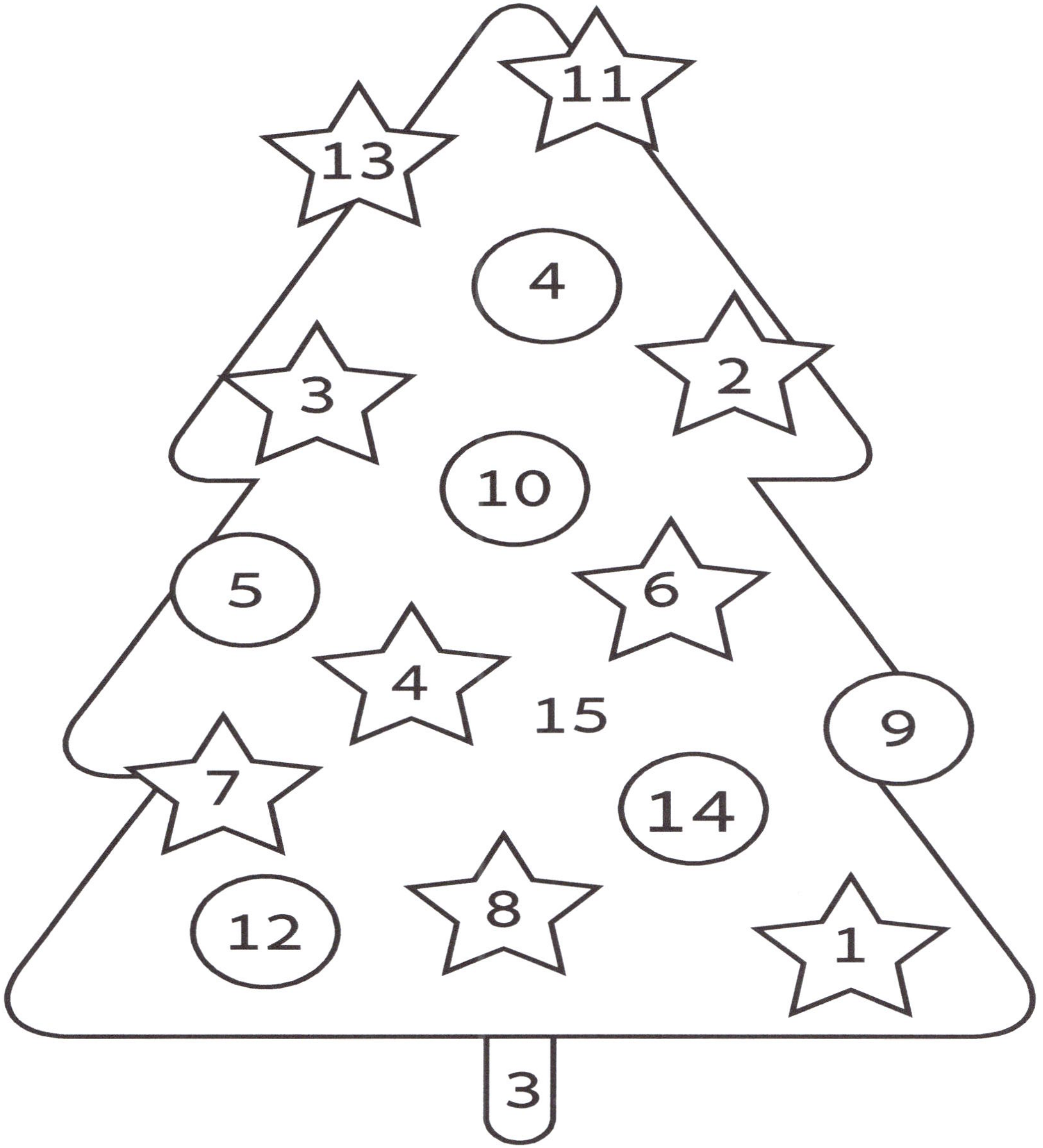

1	blue	
2	grey	
3	brown	
4	yellow	
5	pink	
6	purple	
7	indigo	
8	orange	
9	black	
10	nude	
11	red	
12	golden	
13	silver	
14	lilac	
15	green	

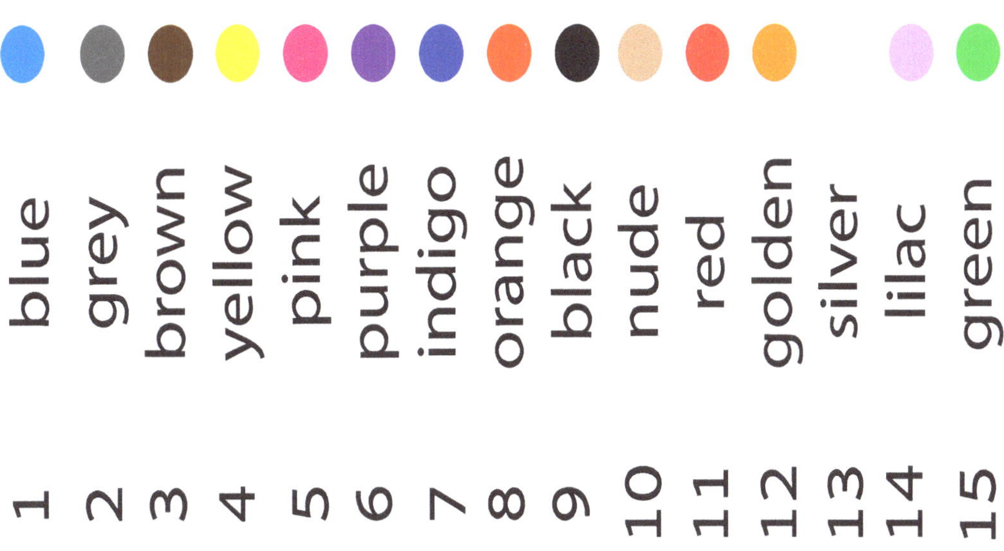

DAY 21

Cut out and glue the game board pieces. Then follow the directions at the top of the page.

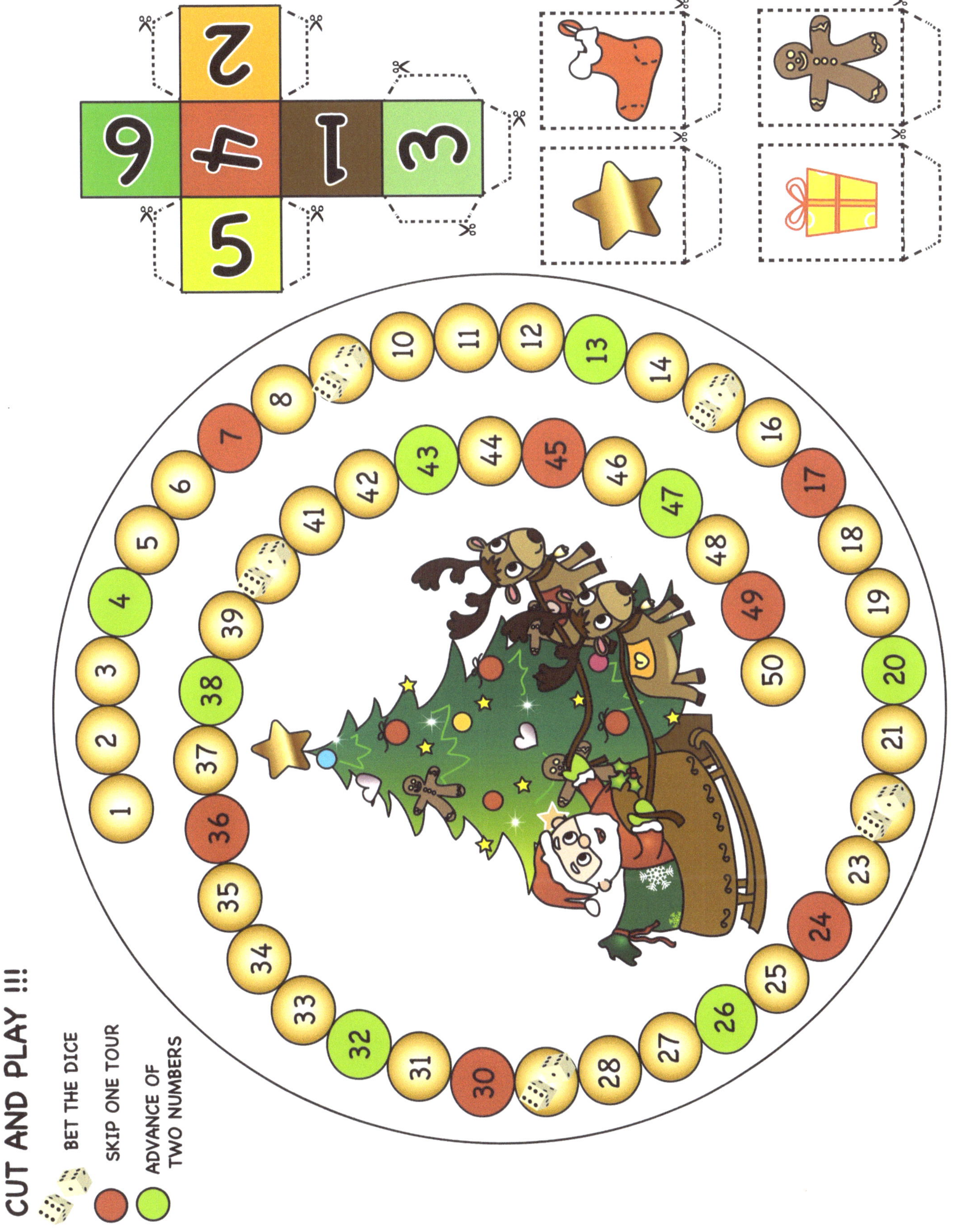

DAY 22

As you find the words in the word search, color the letters with a crayon, marker, gel pen, or colored pencils.

DAY 23

Compare the number of things found in each row.

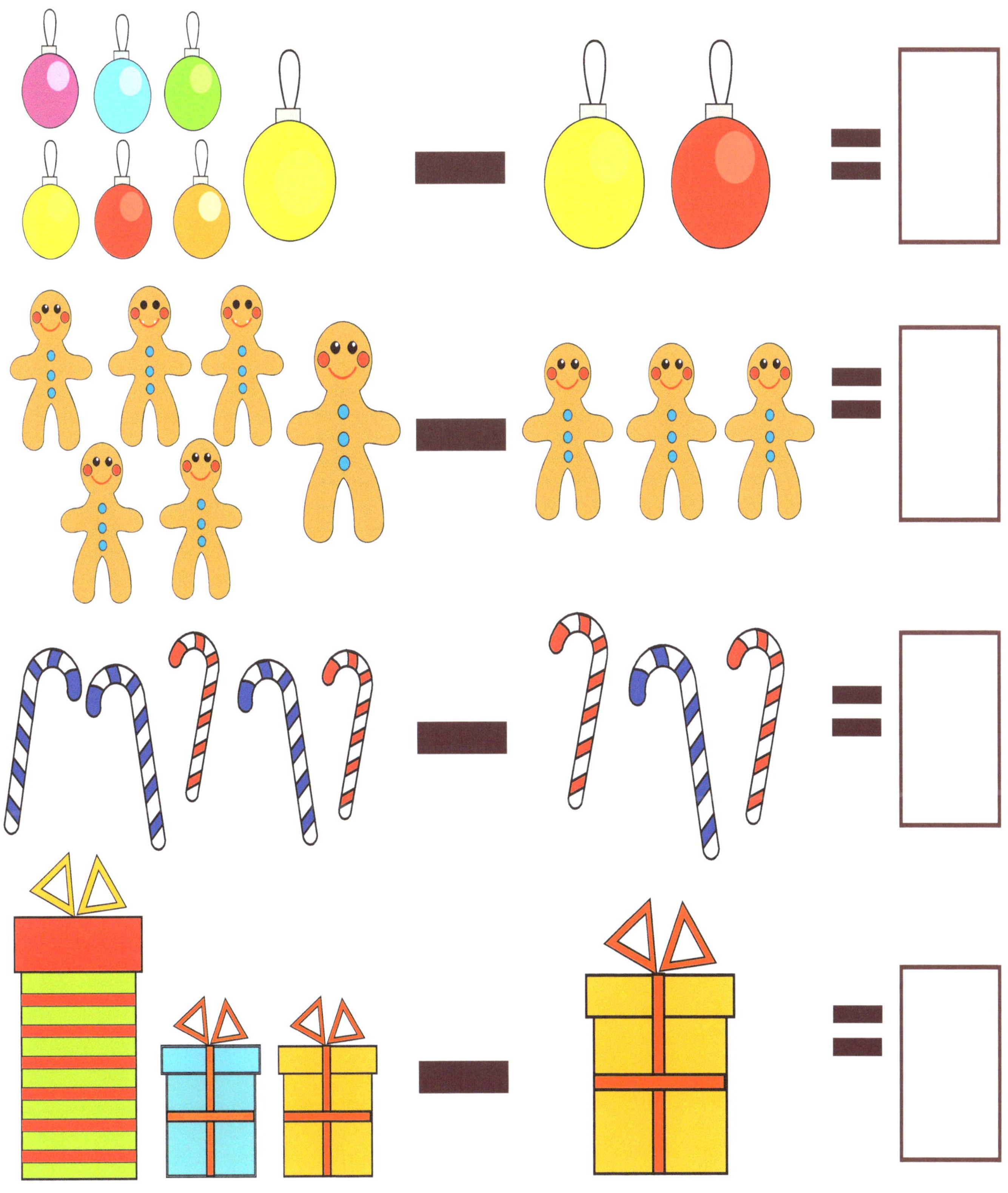

DAY 24

What do the letters spell in this maze?

DAY 25

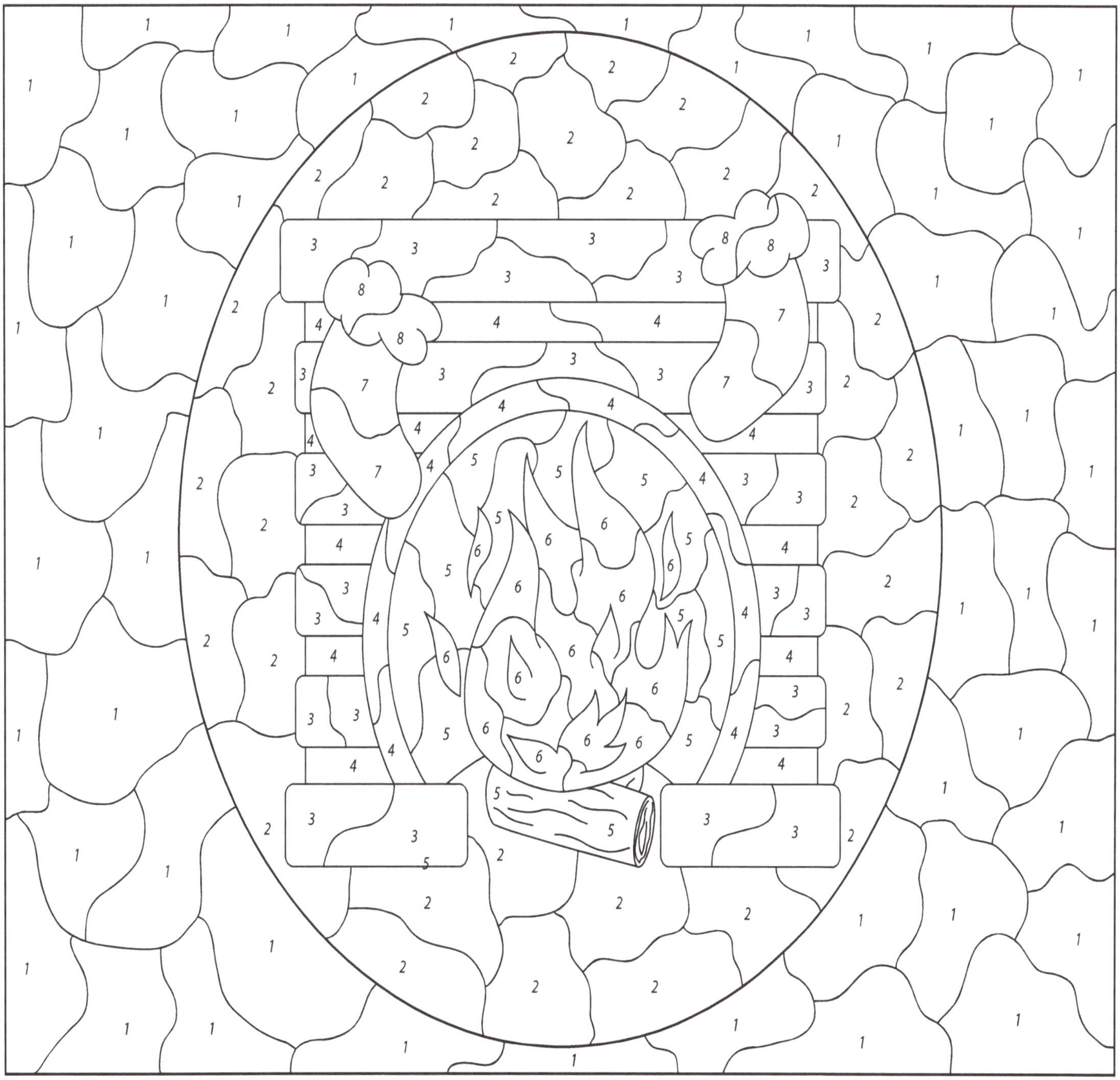

Color by number
to decorate the
holiday fireplace.

A bonus page especially for you!

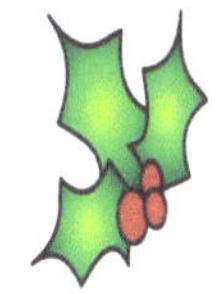

C	S	R	E	B	M	E	C	E	D
C	H	R	I	B	B	O	N	W	E
A	A	R	Y	R	R	E	B	I	K
H	C	R	I	N	T	R	P	N	A
L	A	O	O	S	A	E	I	T	L
E	N	T	M	L	T	D	N	E	F
G	D	C	L	E	S	M	E	R	W
N	L	G	I	F	T	A	A	U	O
A	E	N	A	M	W	O	N	S	N
R	E	I	N	D	E	E	R	S	S

ANGEL
BERRY
CANDLE
CAROLS
CHRISTMAS
COMET
DECEMBER
GIFT
HAT
PINE
RED
REINDEER
RIBBON
SNOWFLAKE
SNOWMAN
WINTER

Find the words (from the list) in the word search to figure out the mystery word!

Extra pictures for nativity scenes!

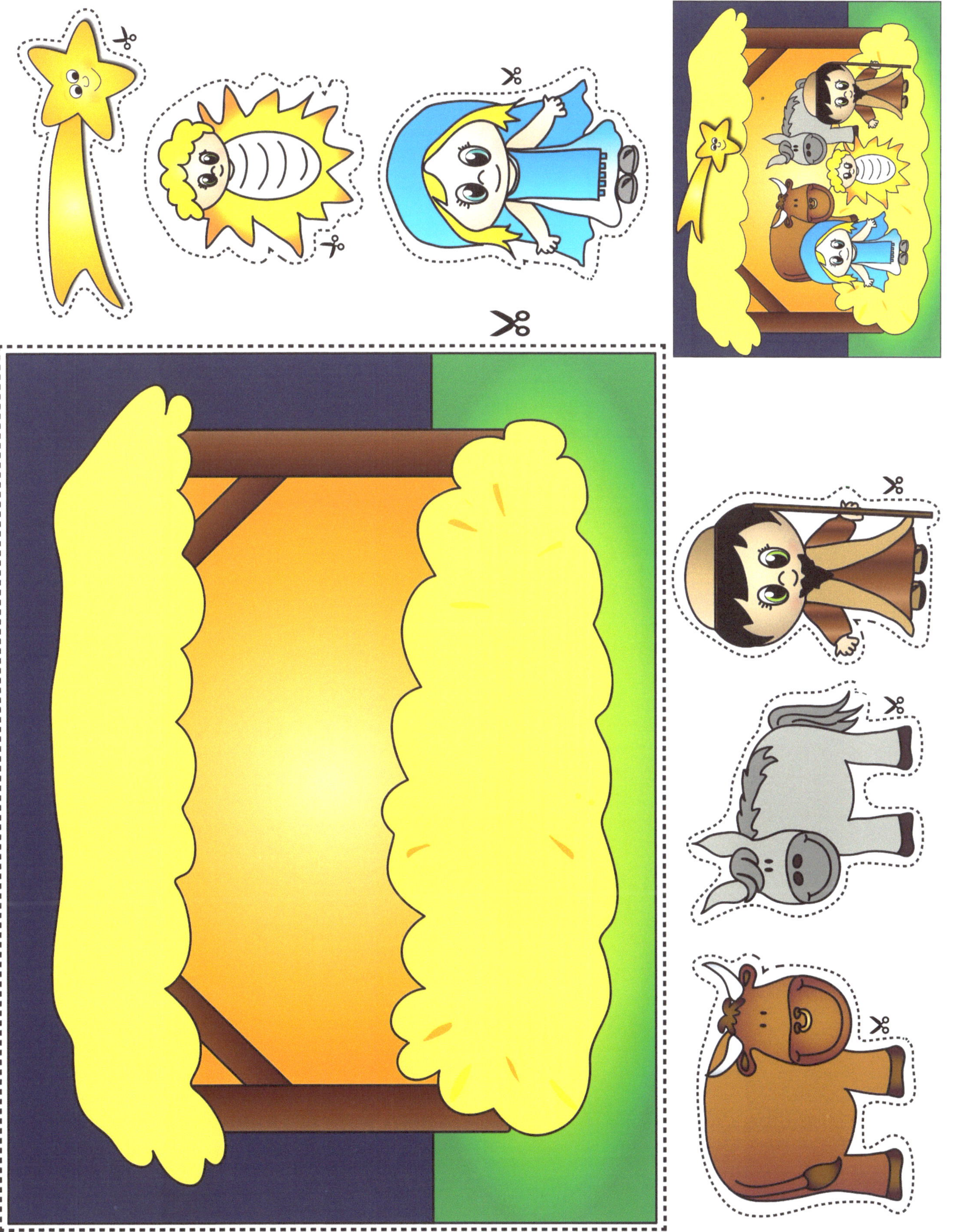

Extra pictures for nativity scenes!

Bonus: Cut out the puzzle pieces. Then glue the nativity puzzle pieces on another sheet of paper.

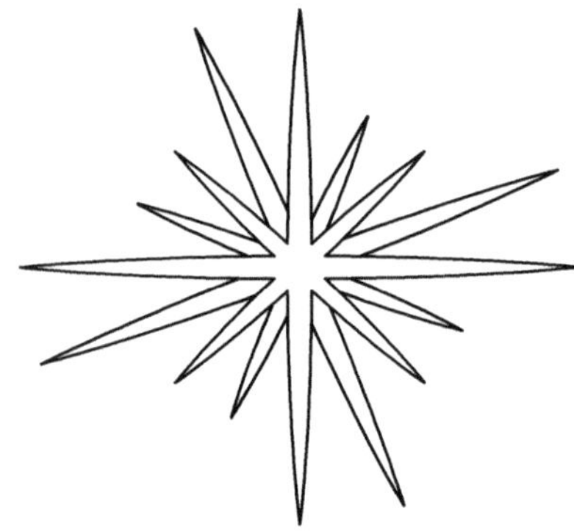

CHRISTMAS ADVENT
ACTIVITY BOOK
For a Very Special
GRANDDAUGHTER!

BY Florabella Publishing 2017
All rights reserved. No part
of this book may be reproduced in any
form or by any electronic or
mechanical means including information
storage and retrieval systems, without
written permission in writing from the
authors. The only exception is by a
reviewer, who may quote short excerpts
in a review.

Granddaughter,
May Your Christmas
Be Merry & Bright!

Florabella Publishing, LLC
florabellapublishing.com